From Territory to Statehood

by Elizabeth Alexander

Scott Foresman
is an imprint of

Glenview, Illinois • Boston, Massachusetts • Chandler, Arizona
Upper Saddle River, New Jersey

ISBN 13: 978-0-328-52539-3
ISBN 10:   0-328-52539-1

4 5 6 7 8   V0FL 16 15 14 13 12

In 1783, when the American colonies won independence from England, the United States was made up of thirteen states along the east coast. Today, fifty states make up the nation.

Of those fifty states, thirty-one were admitted to the Union between 1812 and 1912. This is the story of their journey from territory to statehood.

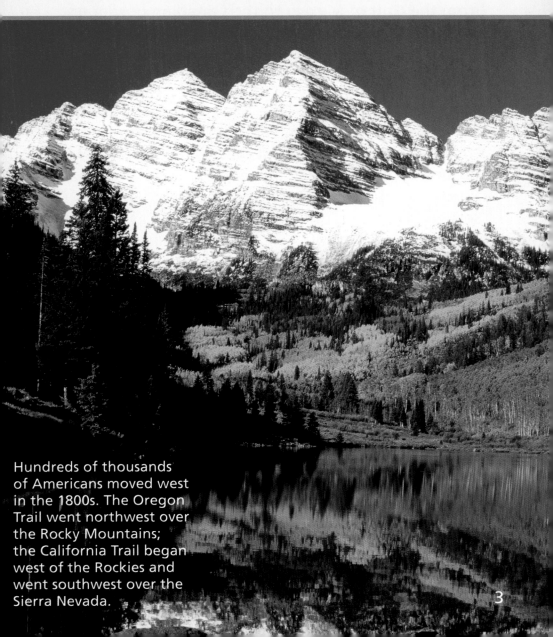

Hundreds of thousands of Americans moved west in the 1800s. The Oregon Trail went northwest over the Rocky Mountains; the California Trail began west of the Rockies and went southwest over the Sierra Nevada.

The Louisiana Purchase

In 1803, President Thomas Jefferson made a deal with France, called the Louisiana Purchase, that doubled the size of the United States. In the Louisiana Purchase, the United States bought more than 800,000 square miles of land for $15 million. That's about 3 cents per acre. The land stretched from the Gulf of Mexico to the Canadian border and from the Mississippi River to the Rocky Mountains.

Winners and Losers

White Americans were delighted by the Louisiana Purchase. Lands west of the Mississippi River, which had belonged to France, were now open to settlers. Native Americans **inhabited** these lands. For many groups, including the Osage and Fox, the Louisiana Purchase meant the loss of their hunting lands to settlers' farms.

The Louisiana Purchase was signed in April of 1803.

A Lasting Legacy

In 1904, one century after the Louisiana Purchase, President Theodore Roosevelt declared it "the event which more than any other, after the foundation of the Government . . . determined the character of our national life." The Purchase would greatly influence white Americans' feelings about whether slavery should be ended or expanded. It put lands inhabited by Native Americans under control of the United States. It gave the United States vast natural resources and paved the way for the young nation's expansion "from sea to shining sea."

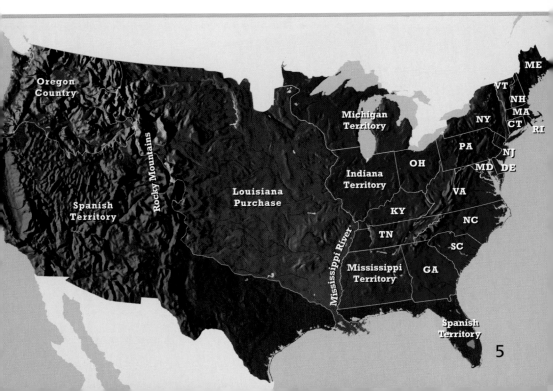

Lewis and Clark

In 1804, Jefferson sent a team to explore the territory gained in the Louisiana Purchase and lands farther west. The President chose his personal secretary, Meriwether Lewis, to lead the **expedition** that would be called the "Corps of Discovery." Lewis invited his friend William Clark to co-lead the Corps of Discovery.

The Mission

"The object of your mission," Jefferson told Lewis and Clark, "is to explore the Missouri river . . . and such principal streams of it, as . . . may offer the most direct and practicable water communication across this continent for the purposes of commerce. . . ." Jefferson had several goals for the mission: to map the territory; to identify its plants, animals, and natural resources; to establish good relationships with Native American leaders; and to prepare the way for American settlers.

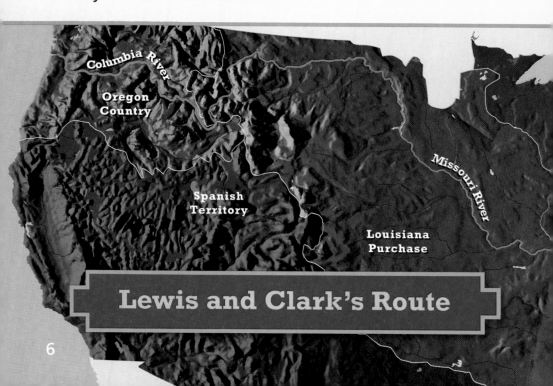

Columbia River

Oregon Country

Spanish Territory

Louisiana Purchase

Missouri River

Lewis and Clark's Route

The Team

The Corps of Discovery was nearly fifty men strong. It included twenty-seven soldiers, a French-Indian **interpreter,** and one enslaved man, York, who was owned by Clark. Lewis's dog, a Black Newfoundland named Seaman, also came along.

Fur trappers and Native Americans helped the Corps of Discovery along the way. A young Shoshone woman, Sacagawea, joined the expedition with her interpreter husband. She showed Lewis and Clark plants that they could eat or use as medicines. Because there was a Native American woman and a child with the expedition, Native Americans believed the Corps when they said they were peaceful. This helped them pass safely through Native American lands in the far West.

Achievements and Aftermath

In less than two-and-a-half years, the Corps of Discovery traveled more than 8,000 miles. The team encountered grizzly bears, mountain goats, pronghorn antelope, and prairie dogs—species unknown back East. It found an overland route to the Pacific Ocean. This knowledge paved the way for American settlement in years to come. The natural environment that the Corps of Discovery explored and the Native American groups that it befriended would be forever changed.

Becoming a State

Usually, a state—or several states—grew out of a territory. A U.S. territory was an expanse of land claimed by the United States. As territories west of the Mississippi River grew in population, they applied for statehood. There was a process to follow—a process that remains in place today.

Two acts passed by Congress are key to the process. In the first act, the enabling act, Congress directs a territory to choose delegates, or representatives, to a constitutional convention. The chosen delegates write a constitution for the proposed state. They generally use existing state constitutions as a model.

When the delegates have finished their work, the constitution is submitted to the people of the territory for **ratification**, or approval. After the constitution is ratified, the territory applies to Congress for statehood.

If Congress approves the territory's application, it passes a second act, called the act of admission. This act is submitted to the people and government of the territory. With their approval, the territory at last becomes a state.

In the 1800s, pioneers traveled crosscountry in wagon trains to establish American settlements in the West. They cleared the land of trees or prairie grass and built cabins using logs or sod.

Statehood and Slavery

The United States acquired present-day Missouri in the Louisiana Purchase of 1803. In 1819, people living in the Missouri Territory applied for statehood. Missouri asked to enter the Union as a slave state—a state where slavery was allowed by law.

When Congress debated Missouri's application, eleven slave states and eleven free states made up the Union. Missouri's admission as a slave state would upset the balance. It would give the slave states a two-vote advantage in the Senate. (Each state sends two senators to Congress.)

James Tallmadge, Jr., of New York warned that Missouri could set a **precedent**, allowing other western territories to join the Union as slave states. Tallmadge led the opposition in the House of Representatives to Missouri's admission as a slave state. Representative Thomas W. Cobb of Georgia led those who supported Missouri's application.

The people of Missouri pushed Congress to face an issue that it had been avoiding as much as possible. Many political leaders, among them former President Jefferson, feared that the Union could be split wide open over slavery.

The slave states, all but Delaware and Maryland, lay in the South. The free states all lay in the North. A failure to resolve the issue of slavery helped lead to civil war between the two regions.

The Missouri Compromise

After much debate, Congress reached a **compromise** in 1820. The Missouri Compromise allowed Missouri to enter the Union as a slave state, and it also formed a new free state, Maine, which was originally part of Massachusetts.

Congress wanted to keep the issue of slavery from coming back when other territories applied for statehood. To achieve this goal, the Missouri Compromise divided the Louisiana Territory. Slavery would be forbidden in new states north of the Missouri Compromise line (shown on the map) and permitted in new states south of the line.

The Missouri Compromise

Oregon Country

Unorganized Territory from Louisiana Purchase

Michigan Territory

Spanish Territory

36°30' Missouri Compromise Line

MO

Arkansas Territory

IL

IN

OH

KY

TN

MS

AL

GA

LA

VA

NC

SC

PA

NY

ME

VT

NH

MA

CT

RI

NJ

MD

DE

Florida Territory

Free states and territories
Slave states and territories
Closed to slavery by Missouri Compromise
Open to slavery by Missouri Compromise
Not U.S. Territory

11

Western States and the Dates They Gained Statehood

Louisiana	April 1812
Indiana	December 1816
Mississippi	December 1817
Illinois	December 1818
Missouri	August 1821
Arkansas	June 1836
Texas	December 1845
Iowa	December 1846
Wisconsin	May 1848
California	September 1850
Minnesota	May 1858
Oregon	February 1859
Kansas	January 1861

Nevada	October 1864
Nebraska	March 1867
Colorado	August 1876
North Dakota	November 1889
South Dakota	November 1889
Montana	November 1889
Washington	November 1889
Idaho	July 1890
Wyoming	July 1890
Utah	January 1896
Oklahoma	November 1907
New Mexico	January 1912
Arizona	February 1912

An Expanding Nation

The United States grew steadily in land area from the Louisiana Purchase of 1803 through the mid-1800s. As more territories became states, the Union expanded west to the Pacific Ocean and south to Mexico.

The Mexican-American War

Texas was part of Mexico for many years before winning its independence and becoming a nation in 1836. By then, tens of thousands of Americans lived in Texas, and at their request, the United States **annexed** Texas in 1845. However, Mexico believed that the United States had annexed land that belonged to Mexico along with Texas. Consequently, Mexico broke off relations with the United States. In 1846, American troops provoked a skirmish with Mexican troops that led to war.

A Costly Victory

The war ranged from the fringes of Mexico into its heartland. After a series of bloody battles—fought with guns, cannons, pickaxes, and crowbars and in hand-to-hand combat—the United States captured Mexico City, ending the war in September 1847. The peace treaty was signed in February 1848.

The United States won land including present-day New Mexico, California, Nevada, Utah, and most of Arizona in the Mexican-American War. The territorial gains were great, but the costs were high. More than twenty-five thousand Mexicans and thirteen thousand Americans died, the latter mainly of disease. In addition, the war revived the dispute over slavery in the territories.

Statehood and Slavery: Issues Resurface

After the Mexican-American War, Congress had to decide whether territories that the United States had won would enter the Union as slave states or free states. The conflict over slavery had become so heated that many people feared civil war was unavoidable.

In 1849, California applied for admission as a free state. A new free state would upset the balance between slave states and free states that had been kept for almost thirty years, since the Missouri Compromise.

Senator Henry Clay of Kentucky had engineered the Missouri Compromise. In 1850, he again took the lead, pleading with Northern and Southern Senators to compromise in order to avert civil war. "I [hope] . . .," Clay declared, "that if the direful event of the [breakup] of the Union is to happen, I shall not survive to behold the sad and heart-rending spectacle."

The Compromise of 1850

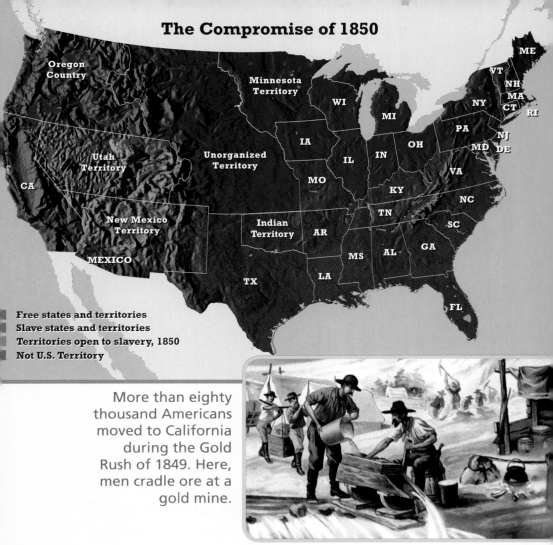

Oregon Country

Minnesota Territory

ME

VT
NH
MA
CT
RI
NY

WI

MI

PA

Utah Territory

Unorganized Territory

IA

OH

MD DE
NJ

IL

IN

VA

CA

MO

KY

NC

TN

New Mexico Territory

Indian Territory

AR

SC

MEXICO

MS

AL

GA

TX

LA

FL

Free states and territories
Slave states and territories
Territories open to slavery, 1850
Not U.S. Territory

More than eighty thousand Americans moved to California during the Gold Rush of 1849. Here, men cradle ore at a gold mine.

The Compromise of 1850

After more than eight months of debate, Congress reached a fragile agreement known as the Compromise of 1850. The compromise allowed California to enter the Union as a free state. However, it did not resolve the issue of slavery. Congress left it to the white inhabitants of New Mexico, Nevada, Arizona, and Utah territories to determine whether to organize themselves as slave states or free states.

The Kansas-Nebraska Act, 1854

- Free states and territories
- Slave states and territories
- Open to slavery

The Kansas-Nebraska Act

Senator Stephen A. Douglas helped engineer the Compromise of 1850. In 1854, he introduced a **bill** to establish the Kansas and Nebraska territories. Douglas's bill broke the rule forbidding slavery in the Louisiana Purchase area north of the Missouri Compromise line. It allowed white settlers in Kansas and Nebraska to decide for themselves whether to allow slavery.

Congress passed the bill, so it became an act of law, known as the Kansas-Nebraska Act. Northerners were furious because the Kansas-Nebraska Act expanded the area that could become slave states, while Southerners were pleased for the very same reason.

Bleeding Kansas

After Congress passed the Kansas-Nebraska Act, northern settlers went into Kansas to prevent slavery. Southern settlers went to establish it. In 1854 and 1855, Southerners who lived in Missouri crossed the border into Kansas and voted—illegally—in territorial elections.

Fighting broke out between armed groups of pro- and anti-slavery forces. People were killed in the violence that took place in "Bleeding Kansas." The territory had become a battleground over slavery.

Breakup and War

In January 1861, most of the Kansas territory was admitted to the Union as a free state. (The boundaries of the territory were changed; western Kansas later became part of Colorado.) Nebraska did not attain statehood until 1867, after the Civil War (1861–1865).

The breakup of the Union proved as "sad and heart-rending" as Clay had feared. Approximately 364,000 Union soldiers and 258,000 Confederate soldiers died in the Civil War, and hundreds of thousands more were wounded.

The Civil War resolved the conflict over slavery and statehood by ending slavery. It did not, however, guarantee African Americans full rights as citizens. The struggle for civil rights would last another one hundred years.

Oklahoma: Two Territories, One State

Oklahoma followed a different path to statehood than other western territories. In the early 1800s, present-day Oklahoma was part of Indian Territory, lands that Congress had pledged to preserve for Native Americans.

White settlers wanted to farm these set-aside lands, and cattle ranchers wanted them for grazing. Both groups pressured Congress to break its pledge to Native Americans.

Settlers poured into Oklahoma after 1872, when the first railroad to cross the territory was completed. They set up farms and ranches, defying laws and treaties. Congress acted, over time, to meet their demands.

In 1890, Congress took land out of Indian Territory to form the Oklahoma Territory. Settlers from the Midwest and the South staked claims in the new territory. Settlers even came from as far away as Europe to claim land.

In 1905, leaders of five tribes—Cherokee, Creek, Seminole, Choctaw, and Chickasaw—tried to save what remained of Indian Territory. They held a constitutional convention, wrote a state constitution, and asked to be admitted to the Union as the state of Sequoyah.

Congress refused. In 1907, it approved a different plan, joining the Oklahoma and Indian territories to form the state of Oklahoma.

From Atlantic to Pacific

Thirty-one states entered the Union in the one hundred years between 1812 and 1912. In 1889 alone, the number of states increased by four. North Dakota, South Dakota, Washington, and Montana all became states at the same time. By 1912, all the areas that had been territories were now states, and the United States now covered all the land from the Atlantic Ocean to the Pacific, and from the Canadian border to Mexico.

As the nation expanded, railroads and roads were built across the country. It became easier to travel and to ship goods. Settlers who lived in far-off areas were now within reach of cities and towns. Living in the West became less challenging, and people continued to move there.

The settlers who helped our country grow had "unbounded push and energy," as Congressional Representative Samuel S. Cox of New York observed. "These [western settlers]," he said, "are the men who have tunneled our mountains, who have delved our mines, who have bridged our rivers, who have brought every part of our empire within the reach of foreign and home markets, who have made possible our grand growth and splendid development. . . . There is no parallel in history to their achievements."

A Flag with Fifty Stars

Arizona became the forty-eighth state in 1912, and for many years no new states were added to the Union. That changed in 1959 when the United States welcomed two new states and added two new stars to the flag.

Alaska was the forty-ninth state. It had been a possession of the United States since 1867, when Secretary of State William H. Seward purchased Alaska from Russia. This purchase was not popular. Few Americans saw much promise in this far northern land. Critics called the purchase "Seward's Folly," and they called Alaska "Seward's Icebox."

Alaska proved to be very important to the nation, however. A gold rush in the late 1800s brought attention to Alaska's mineral wealth. Then, during World War II, Alaska became an important location for military bases. After the war, Alaskans began to work toward statehood in earnest.

In 1946, the Alaska Statehood Association was founded. A 1955 Constitutional Convention wrote a state constitution, which state citizens adopted in 1956. Finally, on January 3, 1959, Alaska was granted statehood. A new star was added to the American flag.

Unlike Alaska, which the United States bought outright, Hawaii was a sovereign nation when the United States began to acquire business interests there in the 1800s. Hawaii was a monarchy. It was ruled by a king or a queen. Finally, the influence of American businesses became so strong in Hawaii that Queen Liliuokalani was forced out of power in 1893.

Hawaii became a republic the next year. By 1898, the United States had annexed Hawaii, and in 1900 Hawaii became a United States territory. The territory produced important crops such as sugarcane and pineapples. It also became home to important military bases. In fact, it was the Japanese attack on Pearl Harbor, on the island of Oahu, that triggered the United States' entry into World War II.

Hawaiians had been interested in statehood even before the war, but after the war they began to work hard to make it happen. Once Alaska became a state, Hawaiians knew that their territory would soon be granted statehood too.

On August 21, 1959, Hawaii became our fiftieth state. When a new United States flag was unfurled on July 4, 1960, it was the same as the flag we fly today, with thirteen stripes and fifty stars.

Now Try This

Imagine that you live in a small town in Pennsylvania in 1840. Your family of four has decided to move west. To make this long and difficult journey, you will travel in a covered farm wagon called a "prairie schooner." Make a list of the supplies and belongings that you will take.

Today, modern families can experience what life was like on the westward journey by taking part in special vacation reenactments.

Here's How to Do It!

Keep the following in mind as you plan what to pack:

- Everything that your family needs to live must be on this wagon. The trip will take several months.
- Everything must fit on the wagon. The inside space is 10 feet long by 4 feet wide.
- Plan carefully. Many pioneers overload their wagons and must throw off treasured belongings and supplies.
- You and your family will need to eat and drink, stay warm, take care of the horses or oxen that pull the wagon, and protect yourselves from weather and possibly bandits. You must be prepared in case someone gets hurt or the wagon needs to be fixed.

1. 125-pound sack of corn meal

2. Warm blankets

3. Spinning wheel

4.

5.

6.

Glossary

annexed *v.* added territory to an existing city, county, state, or nation.

bill *n.* a proposed law.

compromise *n.* resolution of differences in which both sides give something up.

expedition *n.* journey made for a specific purpose.

inhabited *v.* lived in.

interpreter *n.* someone who helps people who speak different languages communicate with each other.

precedent *n.* example used to justify later decisions.

ratification *n.* approval of a proposed constitution or constitutional amendment.